The Stone Serpent

Barates of Palmyra's Elegy for Regina his Beloved

An Eastern Serenade

Nouri Al-Jarrah

The Stone Serpent

Barates of Palmyra's Elegy for Regina his Beloved

Translated from the Arabic by
Catherine Cobham

Banipal  Books

The Stone Serpent,
Barates of Palmyra's Elegy for Regina his Beloved
First published in English translation
by Banipal Books, London, October 2022

Arabic copyright © Nouri Al-Jarrah 2022
English translation copyright © Catherine Cobham, 2022
Original Arabic title:
الأُفعوانُ الحَجَري – مرثية بارات التدمري لمحبوبته ريجينا
Published by Dar al-Mutawassit, Milan, 2022.

A CIP record for this book is available in the British Library
ISBN 978-1-913043-29-2
E-book: ISBN: 978-1-913043-30-8

Front cover image of the tombstone of Regina
© Tyne & Wear Archives & Museums / Bridgeman Images

Banipal Books
1 Gough Square, LONDON EC4A 3DE, UK
www.banipal.co.uk/banipalbooks/

Banipal Books is an imprint of Banipal Publishing
Typeset in Cardo

Printed and bound in Great Britain by Clays Ltd, Elcograf S.p.A.

An Eastern Serenade

CONTENTS

AUTHOR'S NOTE

Who is this adventurer who came from the East to liberate a woman from the West and name her Regina, provocatively, as a challenge to the system of slavery that existed in the Roman Empire? Who is Barates[1] from Palmyra and who is Regina[2] the Celt? A farm worker was turning over the earth in the remains of a Roman fort in the heart of the British Isles, and produced these two names for us. How did a young man tanned by the sun of Palmyra come to put his arm around the waist of a Celtic girl with a red plait, and wander with her over the lush green hills by Hadrian's Wall, down to the River Tyne, where brown men from Nineveh rowed in small boats carrying cargo from the big ships, chanting in sad voices songs that sounded like strange prayers? It is strange too that these men with their strong muscles and brown faces had left behind their boats in the warm waters of the Euphrates and joined the fleets of Septimius Severus, arriving in this cold water in the North, to become labourers and oarsmen in the shadow of a Roman wall that twists like a stone serpent.

Who is Regina, and who is Barates? Archaeologists found the Celtic woman's tombstone in the Roman fort of Arbeia. She had died young, in her thirties, and a few miles away they found the grave of Barates. Everything we know about Barates is also everything we know about Regina, contained in one line that the shattered lover had engraved in Aramaic, his native language, on the Palmyrene-style tomb of the beloved woman. So we know that he freed her from slavery, named her Regina ('Queen'), and she became his lover and his wife, and then he lost her. The hero of this poem did not forget to include his Syrian identity on the tombstone.

A single line fired my imagination, and I, and this poem, are indebted to it.

NJ

2

An Eastern Serenade

If you weren't here
if I hadn't jumped down off this wall that twists
   like a stone serpent[3]
and returned the sword to its owner
could I have stood here in broad daylight
to hear someone calling my name
if you weren't here
if your voice hadn't repeated my name in this
   bare stretch of land.

The waves carried my boat westwards and I
   joined Caesar's[4] army.

Why am I here with these skilful archers[5] on
this wall, with the mist roaming over the slopes
and trees, down to the bend in the river,[6] and
tumultuous waves breaking over the stone
towers, waves that rose and crashed onto
Caesar's land here, land of the Caledonian Celts
and barbarians with their shaved heads and faces
painted with flower dyes?

Were they really barbarians?[7]

When they approached shouting at the tops of
   their voices
falling under the arrows
on their sides
and knees
and faces
were they paying the price of love?

O what a land, more remote than any other land,
as if my gods no longer had eyes to see me.

* * *

I ride around on my horse from Cirta, the cold breeze ruffling his smooth mane, my face buffeted by the breeze soaked with the blood of the plunging hordes of the Tattooed Ones[8]

Those brave fighters from Palmyra string their bows in the forts and towers, and descend in waves on chariots laden with shields and spears and flying banners.

They appear on parade with their thick black eyebrows and faces burnt by a distant sun.

They travel for miles by day and night in dense clouds of green under dark drifting skies, ready to ambush attackers sheltered by the forests, dispatched by nature to translate its passions into bloody rounds of fighting.

* * *

How many slaves from Samos, fighters from
Thrace and stonecutters from Tuscany perished
under the stone slabs brought from the quarries
in the winters of York, just so Hadrian had a
wall where he could hide with his Thracian
lover?[9]

The visiting consul at the door of his tent, two
Macedonian soldiers next to him guarding the
eagle,[10] lets his hawk-like eyes roam over the
battle-ready battalions to compare horseman
with horseman and muscle with sword.

* * *

You who stop to read my words that tremble
with cold, did you arrive here like me on a boat
made of cedar wood from the mountains of
Numidia,[11] or on a raft thrown down from a
ship near a North Sea shore?

I'm not a standard-bearer, but a cloth merchant
   from the East.

If I lay down my sword by the river
may Baal[12] bless my footsteps home
and forgive my sins.

* * *

In the storm, when we'd crossed the Roman
   Sea, I prayed to you, Asherah,[13] for you are
   mistress of these waves

I prayed to you
and made a wish to Baal.

When I saw dry land, I saw you washing your
   feet by the river
I saw the light falling in drops
from your ankle

and I begged El[14] on high to bless the eyes that
   saw you.

* * *

Warriors from Thrace with mariners from
   Nineveh[15] surround the consul in riverboats
all eyes on the estuary
and in the open sea, the ship is waiting.

The commander of the legion beckons to the
   traveller, and his brown Carthaginians,
freed from their shackles by the sword's
   intervention,
fill the horizon with their cries.

* * *

They will all go to the hunt and I will stay
with the women who stripped sackcloth from
the children's bodies and washed their mud-
spattered bottoms with ash and linen,
then a Sicilian slave trader will arrive with
    beardless youths from Delos,[16]
wearing necklaces inlaid with blue stones to
protect them from the eye and accompanied by
a girl dressed in the skin of a wild beast.

How did you capture my heart
just by fixing your dark eyes on mine!

* * *

If you were not here
if you were not the flower that opened at
    twilight
and the perfume that flowed through the deep
    clouds of day
if you were not the sky, and the boat, and the
    shore
and now, the threshold of the house,
and the lamp lighting my way at night

If you were not here
if you were not the flower that opened at
    twilight
and the perfume that flowed through the misty
    dawn.

* * *

How did I climb the wall when the Iberian
　　centurion picked me out in my alien clothes[17]
　　that Baal had blessed?
I became an archer hunting in the heart of the
　　forest
I startled the young Celt
as the hunter's arrow startles its prey.

On stormy nights, when the guards sit by their
blazing fires, the wind mocks me and carries to
my frozen ears the groans of the fighter who
encountered my arrow, and translates his last
words for me.

For whose sake am I standing here among
blacksmiths, skilful sword makers, in the
presence of Alexandrians from Ptolemaic Egypt
spouting their ideas, and Iturean cynics from
Damascus and Yabroud,[18] and Carthaginian[19]
giants from distant Cirta?[20]

* * *

No palm tree here
nor cedar
not even an olive tree lighting up the hill!

* * *

I was fleeing from the blaze of the sun into the
    shadow of Baal Shamin[21]

I thank the driver of the clouds
because he has poured rain into the soil
and dripped honey into the heart of the fields

I sing my hymn to Baal:
I will build you a house
the like of which the heavens have not seen,
a palace where no king on earth has dwelt
and no prince set foot.[22]

* * *

How can I, Barates, my face tanned by the sun
of Tadmur, reach you in the deep heart of
silence and the oblivion of sleep, how can I
rescue you from the forest of wolves, I who
wander with my Damascus linen and cotton
through towns and villages that run from the
clamour of infantry, the clashing of swords, the
turmoil of fleets on the river?

How can I retrieve you from the silence of the
forest and the river's wilderness?

How can I?

How can I?

If I could, then you could sing with me the
poem I carried on pink marble when I left
Tadmur[23] for Damascus and reached Tyre[24] in
chains and was put on a boat with a sail, and
in the turmoil of boats the spectre of Baal
descended from the mountainous wave and
loosened my chains and delivered me to the
mistress of the sea; so that you could be the

woman to whom the Greek poet wrote his
Syrian poem,[25] and I could be the Wanderer,[26]
searching for Suha[27] and Suhail.[28]

* * *

You could have been
mine
with spindle and wool
and I could have had a bed in a room
and wood by a fireside.

Even if Suetonius[29] had not used Nero's sword
   on Boudicca's neck[30]
and the boats had not arrived with builders from
   Alexandria to map out the land and cut
   through the plains and the forests with stones
you could have been mine, a joyful breeze
   blowing over the land of my day,
your reckless eyes delighting
at my footsteps
I, Barates, returning from the river with a
   shimmering fish.

* * *

If I had been Hercules, on a battlefield in a
    shaking chariot
with a rainbow disturbing the light[31]
would I have challenged the guardian of the
    waters,[32]
or turned a blind eye to him
and let him hide in the depths of the well?

* * *

Who set fire to the granaries: was it the young
men of the northern tribes coming down from
the mountains, or the wicked Mycenaean
storekeeper who found beetles in the jars of
wheat?[33]

What wild fantasy could make a follower of
Esus,[34] slain by an arrow that filled his
throbbing chest with blood, perform the
function of a beetle in a Roman cellar!

Who wrote the report and made the soldiers
    gasp in astonishment,
and mock,
if it wasn't the same dissolute Calabrian youth[35]
who bends over the consul's bed every morning
to pour rosewater from a copper jug into two
pink palms, a blue bead hanging from his neck?

* * *

How did I exist?
What did the world look like
before you set foot on the earth
and I set eyes on you?

Before that shackled foot ensnared me?

* * *

The mist kills bows and archers
the mist devours stones, and walls, and wanders
    over the river,
and those who dropped from forts, pelted with
    hatchets and axes,
fell into the pit of winter.

The souls of the fallen wander over the treetops.

The wooden chariots with wheels sinking
into the grass all winter, their iron rims studded
with snails and in their empty insides wriggling
worms replete with the dampness
of the earth, black,
weighed down by the rain,
the chariots plunge downhill and crash and fall
  apart, they and the fighter with his Iturean
  spear,[36]
leaving above them the shriek of the wind
and the hills in shock.

At the bottom,
deep down,
at the bottom,
the fighter let out his last sigh.

Only the worms remained lively
while the bodies crumble
and collapse
at the site of the massacre
as if,
writhing in the fading light of day,
they are the last sign of the times.

The mist drifts over the little forts
and over the random inscriptions and over time,
whenever tumult erupts on the wall and calm
    deals it invisible blows.

* * *

And now
in April
the grass grows higher
and twists
and grows wilder
in the empty spaces,
plants climb over the wreckage of chariots
and bodies.

A pale sun unearths the skeletons of fighters
and wind, wind, wind,
wind blows from the north over skulls split by
   axes
and bloody fragments,
in cracks steeped in silence and moistened by
   the air
an adolescent light
has begun to play with the pale yellow flowers
   so small they are almost invisible . . .

With their saliva and feelers small creatures
absorb the microbes from the wreckage.

Is there an ending wiser and stronger than the
   wreckage last winter left on the plain
when the sun shines on the little thing and it
   devours the big things
and all-embracing calm rushes to make peace
   with raging nature in the sight of death and
   its works?

* * *

Where are the archers of Palmyra who filled
   ears and ages with their joyful cries?
Where are their stories that the wind rolled all
   along the wall?

Their blazing fires in swirls of mist sent fragrant
   smoke into the forests,
and lit up the axes of the Tattooed Ones,
   approaching to commit suicide, like salmon,
   in the middle of the day.

Whenever the forest opened its mouth and
spewed out another wave of bleeding hairy legs
and wounded shoulders, skulls went ahead of
them to be houses for the snails of the time.

* * *

In which languages did the wounded address
their gods as they drew their last breaths and
deposited them in cracks in the ground?

White wolves prowling smelt their blood,
which shimmered in the sun of the short days
before drying on their bodies under skies that
darkened as they witnessed the slaughter.

Odin[37] was not there on a ladder or in a fort:
perhaps he was playing with the youths on the
riverbank and hiding in the mist in the forests;
he will never appear on the low ground before
another massacre in another winter unless the
last fighter calls out to the rock sculpted by the
wind.

* * *

The fire your hand sent down, Septimius, to
devour the woods, meadows and fields of maize,
and drive the Caledonians barefoot into the
caves of the north, came back on the wind and
with its blazing wings set your imperial coffin
alight.

It melted the eagle on your ring and the chain
of gold where a jeweller from Antioch engraved
the name "Julia" next to your Phoenician name
that had terrified the aristocrats of Rome.[38]

Where are the banners that led the battalions of
the Praetorian Guard on the way from
Damascus to Tyre, when the sails were hoisted
on the boats sailing in the sun to Eboracum?

What will Jupiter say to Caracalla when he
looks down from his horse and sees your body
burning on the water?[39]

* * *

Fifty thousand young men from distant
provinces were swallowed by the dragon with
its seven heads looking behind and before:
craftsmen, farmers, shepherds and hunters
appeared in coats of armour carrying shields and
flaunting shiny helmets whose red crests
captured the hearts of country girls.

Conscripts from Egypt of the Ptolemies,
Iturians from Syria, and Africans, all were
fighters in the battle, daredevil Spartans too.
The teeth of the forests ground their bones,
and the rains and floods buried them.[40]

O delusions of grandeur!
And fiery blaze after the eloquence of the
   sword!

* * *

The driver of the clouds[41] led my footsteps from
  the blue of summer to the wildness of winter!
The daughters of the dew and girls of the mist,[42]
who lay down with Baal in my field,
left me here bewildered!

The sky poured forth dew, and the stars
  awakened the wormwood and filled the air
  with perfume.

With you I reached the source of the two
rivers[43] and walked in the sun of my days; so
why did you accept my vows, since you were
going to forsake me and let the dust snatch
from me the only thing a stranger had left in
the world?

★ ★ ★

I made my room a tent for the god, so why did
the gods not hear the sound of my heart?

* * *

It was not a dream, nor a flash of
   unconsciousness, when the sky split in two,
   and the eagle swooped down on the snake.[44]
You were laid out on the damp leaves of poplar
   trees and the seven youths were guarding
   your sleep.[45]

* * *

Nothing resembles the silence of your slumber
   but the silence of the air in the lungs of the
   forest
when the mist spreads and swallows up the
   towering trees
and descends to engulf me so I no longer see
   my feet, nor my steps on the ice of my days.

* * *

The mist brushes my face, and the mist leads me
    astray,
so let me go far away, and hear the sound of
    horses' hooves, and she-camels ambling,
and glimpse through the palm leaves vague
    shapes of riders,
swirling dust burning me and filling my eyes,
let me join those who have already gone, and
    stand up and greet the summer of the south,
as the hot noon wind blows and the sand stings
    my face.

* * *

My blood is the trembling of a wounded wolf,
and my voice the howl of a forest on fire.

* * *

Your voice that disturbs the sleep of the gods has
*   roused me from my slumber*
your voice breaks the darkness
and descends
to demand my hand from the marble of death.

You let me hear your voice
so I could hear
and you gave me your hand
so I could stand up.

*Let me stand up then, and walk with you towards
the river
and all day long see the hills rising and the sun
floating on the water.
I am not a princess from the East, and I have never
strolled with a young man in the gardens of Rome
but I have slept beside you
under laughing clouds
so I may draw from your hand that plucked the
mulberries for me the thorn that hurt my hand.*

* * *

I am the woman whom the eagle snatched from the
 forest
and when you saw her
on that very day you gave her the hill and the river
 and the fleeing fish.

Even Esus, who witnessed my birth,
and always sent Lenus[46] after me with his rams
 flaunting their horns and Maponus[47] with his
 strange melodies to drive the beast away from me,

even Esus was not the one to name me.

You named me.

So I exist.

* * *

Your voice precedes your footsteps over the ground
  of my sleep
and your brown palm fills my shirt
so let me sleep then
calmly
and be the flower of unconsciousness in the forest of
  sleep.

* * *

The lakes beyond the hill sigh and groan, and
the little pools of water in the heart of the
forest weep over your foot
and your steps that hurt the spring wandered all
around, they and the little flowers frightened
by the darkness . . .
The little branches shake
the sun's ray grows gloomy
and the cold winds roar and crash
and rage . . .
My gods do not see me
My gods are blind, and do not see, and this
spring is the wreckage of footsteps on ground
that is cracking apart.

The mist attacks, the mist roams over the slopes,
the mist devours the winter firewood and the
dusty path behind the house, the mist brings
down its axe and shatters my back, my eyes are
two hunted animals and my body a dark pit in a
dark winter . . .

And arrows
fill
the pit.

* * *

Could I have existed
if you weren't here, Regina?
If I weren't Allat's[48] gift to the soul of the forest,
   and you the joy of light after the gazelle's
   caprices?
Could I have freed your hand from the eagle's
   claw,
and offered my palms to your winged foot,
and my swift horse to the wild rocking of your
   hips,
if I were not the man from Palmyra who
   exchanged linen for a sword
and gave his heart to Baal to be a sacrifice?

London, 9 April 2021

After

An Eastern Serenade

Voices and Songs

Regina's Song by the River

If I had a sister to comb my hair
I wouldn't need a river or a mirror

Let's wait for the boats of summer
Barates said
for in the boats of summer the Phoenician
    merchants will arrive
and in their crates of wares the shiniest mirrors,
    made in the markets of Sidon,
brass and glazed enamel
with lapis lazuli frames,
and a pouch of gazelle skin and an engraved
    amulet of Poseidon

I look at my face in the water
and see you,
with your yellow braids, your wet eyelashes,
Saitada[49]
Saitada

If I had a sister to comb my hair,
as water flowed beside us
I wouldn't need boats and mirrors
and Phoenicians and their crates of wares in
    summer.

The Archer from Palmyra

Today I will not go up to the temple.
I have no vows for Jupiter, or even Baal.
What am I to do with gods who've never
  satisfied my desire
for answers to my questions?

I gave a quarter century of my life to this biting
  wind,
far from the sun of Palmyra,
I drew my bow to wound the painted
  Caledonian youth with my winged arrow
but I descended from the wall
with pains in my knees
and a few drachmas that wouldn't even get me
  to Londinium on the river
so I'll curse
night and day
and let my gods hear me and die of rage,
since I will never have, even in a dream, a boat
  to take me to Baniyas.[50]
Most likely I will die here and be buried by this
  stupid wall,
and not see Syria again.

Do you expect me, the warrior who wasted his
    life in a forest consumed by mist,
to correct the repeated errors of my useless
    gods?

The Birth of the Painted Warrior

Everything they told us by the fireside, those
   whom we buried in the distant hills,
the earth will give to us in summertime.
We crossed the hills to get white limestone
then down through the gorges to where the
   river meanders
and a fish
meanders
in
the river
There we will dye with purple the young man's
   neck,
he was tiny and in the woman's arms
   Morrigan[51] gave him her warning glance and
   Odin[52] cared for him,
and when he grew muscles, he acquired a spear
   and began to go out after Odin into the forest.

I set fire to the oak tree, and saw its tongues of
   flame blue.

All that was left to me of the deer
was its anklebone
I ground it on a stone and mixed it with ash.

Come, Lenus, and see the cheek of the young
  man who has grown and become graceful
Come, you who are clothed in tree bark, and be
  his intercessor in the storms

From the sumac tree, sister of the trees of the
  rocky ground, we brought back glowing
  yellow dye

We rubbed your beating chest with it and let it
  glow
But the purple under your young eyelid was a
  gift from the worm dried in the summer sun.

We'll gather flowers for you from every plain
  and hill
and when they dry, and the wind plays with
  them
we'll grind them in mortars

and until the mountaineer descends with lapis
  lazuli
to fill your face, shoulders and ankles with
  colour
and the calves of your legs,
we'll sing to Odin so you become what he
  wants you to become.
Then two wings will flutter on the boy you
  used to be, and a bird will vanish into a forest
  of hazelwood.

The warrior will emerge from the forest.

News of Boudicca

Where did Boudicca disappear to after the battle
of Watling Street?
Did she go into the river and become a fish, or
climb the hill and turn into an eagle?
The wounded man escaping from captivity saw
her in a wooden cage on a chariot heading for
the sea
and the shepherd who heard a voice coming
from a cave and saw rabbits vanish into their
burrows
said it was Boudicca . . .

The woman, flogged because she was the
queen,
and when the forest and hill obeyed her
wounded call,
she sent her brave knights after the Roman
battalions
and cut out the tongues that licked virgin blood
from the thighs of her daughters.

She destroyed two of Nero's campaigns
and burnt Romans in three cities
not sparing a single cow
or child.

The men of the Iceni,[53] roaming over plains and
   through forests,
lit up their bodies with colours,
and at a look from her eye, keen as the eye of a
   hawk,
they sent their young men to the Roman stables
   armed with fireballs.

Sculptors left no trace of her in stone
no sign of her was found in any book
All the glory went to Agricola,[54]
and were it not for this Italian general, nothing
   would be known of Boudicca.

Nouri Al-Jarrah

A Roman Elegy

Hadrian's Elegy for his beloved Antinous, drowned in the Nile

Your bare foot is silt, and your waist a traveller
 in the light
your waist in the images
Nile
cuts through the song
and descends
from the sky.

While the invaders climb up to conquer the lake
eternity is silt.
And as the skipper shouts to the river, your foot
 is the sun sparkling in a boat.

* * *

I sleep and wake in your heart,
and I sleep to become an idea
no more
than
a torn conscience, and your hands joined
 together.

The first cataract and the sixth cataract, the
  impossible battle,
the pitcher of water poured into the hand of
  Antinous, his image drowning in the water.
The sister weeping at home,
the mother buried in the heart,
the foot, again, in the boat,
rushing water, still water, beams of sunlight
  fleeing over the water.

* * *

I know where the little crocodiles hide in the
  river
but how can I find the foot of Alexander?[55]
All I know is that crocodiles, even the little
  ones, mourn you.

* * *

Nile descends to earth in the company of the
  sky

and youths hurry with pots of ink and henna
 and writing tablets[56]
– Who are you, who are you, who are you?
– I'm the sleep of the one who slept, and he was
 my lover
a moon like a river crossed by the bridegroom's
 hand in the morning
and in the evening it became a bed.

I am the water verse, the *ayah* of water, and with
 every stroke of an oar a burning sun is mine
and boats
in
the sun.

The boats return thirsty from the high seas
and in the afternoon the foam rejoices.

Who are you, if not a procession of young men
returning from the annual games, surrounded
by fields of cotton and reed beds, youths of
paint pots and inkwells for the king's
entertainment,[57] crowned in laurel from
Damascus, entrusted with papyri on cedar wood
rollers brought post haste by peasants who flew

in sandals sewn from buffalo hide over fields
ploughed by the whips of the sun.

Nile sees me passing in a cloud
Nile sees you with me.
Nile purifies itself in the eye of those who see it

– Who are you? Who are you?
said the reckless branch to the fleeing breeze
– I am the footstep seized from behind a tree
beauty worshipped,
the soul buried in the images.

The Tongue of Fire

The Ruin[58]

How shall I fill the void between the aqueduct
   and the bathing pool next to the fort?
Here behind the basalt walls the warriors
washed off the blood and mud, and near them
slave traders arrived in boats across the river and
loosened the chains from the slaves' ankles and
their bloody wrists,
so they could sweeten the market air.

* * *

On rainy mornings a gaggle of young
   merchants stroll around the stables
observed by those who were watching boys
   feeding the horses

And now
no shadow
and no horses neighing

How shall I fill this silence and the void beyond
   it
between the slanting staircase on the stone wall
  of the fort and the foot that trod the wicker
  steps

and broke
and fell
with the man who slipped and fell
and sent his cry into the gloom of the abyss?

* * *

The one who shone, there in the empty space in
  the line,
where the tongue of fire extended to damage
  the parchment and disturb the reader.
The act of creating a void is a skill more ancient
  than the act of construction

a void after a line,
and a void after a word
a void
in
a void
and a void that makes space for the towering
  structure
to
C
O
L
L
A
P
S
E
piece
by piece

So behind the storms the time of the song
was consumed by fire.

Julia Domna's Missing Fingers

The handmaid's thoughts after
the palace massacre

How many times will Caracalla plunge his
    sword into the guts of the soldier who severed
    the empress's fingers?[59]
"The intention was to kill the brother
not to mutilate the mother's hand . . ."
Thus wrote the historian in the entry for that
    day.

What a scandal, for the empress to appear at the
    banquet with three fingers missing.

Even if Caracalla sends the guilty soldier to
    throw himself off a mountain
nothing will change!

As for her, the mistress of Rome descended
    from Syrian nobility,
she will not look round to see her fingers
    amputated and strewn across the marble,

nor the blood that flowed and stained the
   couches.
Her body that sensed a brother's blade on a
   brother's throat
suddenly went numb,
nothing was left alive in her senses
except that painful contraction in her womb.

Your fame that made Rome's legislators greet
   Septimius with a laurel wreath
dissolved in the cup of the killer son like a
   colocynth seed.

And now,
where have the handmaids gone, on the night
   of the two brothers,
with the severed fingers of Julia Domna?

The Edict of Caracalla
212 AD

What shocking blow, what faraway vision seen
    from a hill
with a sudden gesture,
a sign no greater than the finger of a young
    man in a purple cloak,
a brown man, born to a Carthaginian father and
    a Syrian mother,

All who even yesterday were foreigners in
    Rome were changed to Roman citizens.
How will the horrified aristocrats behave after
    today?

Will the barbarian walk alongside the patrician,
    jostle his shoulder and say: I'm Roman too!

And will those shocked by the news
be able to bear the sight of worshippers of El
    and Asherah gathering in the agora[60]
and cheering the imperial edict carved on
    stones,

delighted by those obscure lines,
nodding their heads like us, us Romans,
as if they could read Latin too!

Today, in the afternoon, when they arrive at
    the senate
Syrians, Armenians, Egyptians, Illyrians, men
    from Nineveh
and with them some barbarians from Britannia,
will these strangers in their colourful clothes sit
    in the patricians' seats?
What will they tell the audience and what
    language will they speak?
Will they have a say in the affairs of
    government?

And afterwards, when the patricians recover
    from the blow,
where will those shocked men go to offer
    sacrifices to their gods,
when the Syrians in the markets and temples of
    Rome
have given Jupiter Baal's horns and made
    Aphrodite into Ishtar?

With a sudden gesture, deliberate or improvised
   we still don't know,
everything is changed in this empire

Was it the piercing gaze of an eagle who circled
   high above and saw everything?
or an Eastern coup d'état,
belated revenge for a brown queen buried in
   the forest[61] after Palmyra was reduced to
   ruins?

Who suggested this astonishing idea?
Papinian the jurist from Homs or Caracalla in
   search of more taxes for his treasury?

Yesterday the bewildered patricians with blue
   blood in their veins repeated:
Which river flows through Rome today?
The Tiber or the Orontes?

Caracalla released the eagle from the hill
and answered the question:
Since all roads lead to Rome
let any chariot come to Rome on any of those
   roads.

NOTES

1 British historians and archaeologists believe that Barat or Barates or Bir 'Ata from Palmyra may have been a cloth merchant who somehow arrived on the island of Britain. We think for our part that he may have been taken prisoner or lost his way at sea while engaged in his trade and ended up in Britannia [Roman Britain]. Some think he may at some point have been one of the hundreds of Syrian archers sent to help defend Hadrian's Wall, built on the orders of the Roman emperor Hadrian in AD122, and that when Barates retired he lived in an area close to the main fort on the wall. Roman military law only allowed high-ranking officers to take their families with them to the places where they served.

Soldiers from the East who were demobilized after 25 years' service did not return to the distant countries from where they had been sent to serve in the army, as there were no budgets to allow for that. They often settled where they had served and formed relationships with women from the British tribes and established families with them, and this was the case with Barates who married Regina.

Mary Beard, professor of classics at the University of Cambridge, notes that Roman merchants poured over the eastern Mediterranean, taking advantage of the trading opportunities that followed the conquest, from the slave trade and the spice trade to contracts for military supplies. She thinks that perhaps the Syrian merchant travelled with them on their way back to Rome or Gaul or neighbouring provinces, but we believe this does not preclude the possibility that Barates himself was an archer at some point before he retired from the service, and then became a cloth merchant, taking advantage of the relationships he had forged during his service on the wall, particularly since Syria had an advanced textile industry and well-developed trade.

2 In 1878 archaeologists discovered a tombstone near Arbeia fort, in what is now South Shields, east of Newcastle upon Tyne. Arbeia was important as it guarded the main sea route to Hadrian's Wall and also served as a supply base. The tombstone was in the Palmyra style (1.3m high and 70cm wide) and was described subsequently by scholars as a wonderful and unique ancient artifact. The great surprise was that the sculpture contained Roman Latin and Syrian Aramaic writing, prompting research into the reasons for the existence of this tombstone in the vicinity of a Roman fort in the area of Hadrian's Wall and close to the mouth of the River Tyne. The sculpture – and in our description here we are relying on the mainly English sources we have found useful – "represents a woman in a pose that suggests she was of high status in her time: a long elegant skirt and tunic, her chest ornamented with a necklace and bracelets on her wrists. In her lap is a spindle of wool and beside her a basket containing balls of wool. At her right hand is a jewel box. An expensive memorial indeed!" If we look down, we see clearly the following Latin phrase: "Regina, freedwoman of Barate, alas". This was written using the common Latin abbreviations of the day. Under

the Latin inscription, and as if Barates wanted to declare his pride in his Syrian identity, we read the same phrase in Palmyrene Aramaic: RGYN' BT HRY BR'T' HBL. The Latin inscription contains the name of Barates as the one who erected this tombstone: "to the dear, beloved, liberated [meaning that she had been a slave], lamented for her youth, Regina, 30 years old, from the Catuvellaunian tribe."

Archaeologists required a specialist in Palmyrene Aramaic to read what was written and its implications were thrilling and confusing at the same time. What was a Syrian from Palmyra doing here in this cold wasteland thousands of kilometres away from his homeland in the East? How did he get here? And how did he meet the woman whom he liberated and called Queen and married? And how did it happen that she died young and then he erected this tombstone for her? Who carved this original work of art with its distinctive Palmyrene identity? And where did Barates get the money to pay for work like this, which would have been very costly at that time? Moreover, how did this woman who was not free before she met Barates become rich and own a box of jewels? These are the questions that have puzzled us, and scholars before us. Many of them remain unresolved to this day, making scholars pose the big question: was Barates the only Syrian in this region? Searching for an answer leads scholars to explore further the history of Hadrian's Wall itself and the Roman garrison stationed in its forts, and the nature and circumstances of the Roman military presence in that era.

The sculpture is on display today at the Arbeia Roman

Fort and Museum in the coastal town of South Shields at the mouth of the River Tyne in the north east of England. The story of Arbeia, or the Arab fort, may throw more light on the tale of Barates and Regina, which we believe is the oldest example of economic migration to Britannia when it was a province of both military and civil importance to the Roman empire.

Regarding the artistic and linguistic style of the tombstone, Judith Weingarten, archaeologist and researcher in Palmyrene history and culture at the British School in Athens, believes it is based on a typical Palmyrene formula for honouring the dead: name + lineage or description + elegy. She also considers that the Aramaic text inscribed on the stone stele to Regina is grammatically eloquent, and carved by someone with a knowledge of Latin, which suggests that the general form of the memorial was the work of a sculptor who was possibly Syrian. Now who did Barates think was going to read this tombstone? And who was Barates addressing by writing these strange letters that could only be read by Syrians? The answer is simple in our view, when we learn that Barates was not the only Syrian in the area. (See note 5 below on Hadrian's Wall and the Syrian archers.)

To sum up: Regina – the Roman pronunciation was *Raygeena* – came from the Catuvellauni, a tribe that lived around St Albans in the south of Hertfordshire, about 22 miles north of central London, and was probably sold by her poverty-stricken family and transferred north, as was the case with many impoverished Catuvellaunian families.

3 Hadrian's Wall is a solid stone structure, 127 km long, six metres high and six metres thick. Built by the Roman emperor Hadrian in the year 122, it extends from sea to sea across what is today called England. At intervals along the wall, the Romans built watchtowers, small forts (mileforts), seventeen larger forts and fortified gates. The remains of the wall and the fortifications are still there today. This wall is the second of three walls and the most important. The first was built on the Gask Ridge, in present-day Scotland, and the last was the Antonine Wall, called after Antoninus Pius, built to be the northern border of the Roman Empire, and extending about 63 km and varying in height between three and five metres. A deep trench was dug on its northern side. Construction began in the year 142 and continued for twelve years. Under pressure from warring tribes, the wall was abandoned eight years later, and the Roman garrisons were transferred to Hadrian's Wall.

The three walls were built to repel the raids of the northern Caledonian tribes that inhabited the land of Scotland. These walls had security, military and geographical objectives. They marked the frontiers of the Roman empire and represented its growing colonial presence. In the year 400 British tribes managed to expel the last Roman soldier from the island, and from then on Hadrian's Wall no longer had any defensive function.

4 This does not refer to Julius Caesar, but to the emperor Septimius Severus, born in Leptis Magna (al-Khums in present-day Libya) to a Phoenician father and an Italian

mother. With his second Syrian wife, Julia Domna, he was the founder of the Syrian dynasty in the Roman Empire.

5 English historical and archaeological sources suggest that 500 skilled Syrian archers, originally from Palmyra, were stationed along Hadrian's Wall and formed part of a garrison of infantry and cavalry of 8,000 men. Only 20 percent of the Roman forces along the wall were of Italian origin, and the rest were brought from the eastern provinces of the empire, from different peoples belonging to the Mediterranean basin, North Africa, the Adriatic, and the Iberian peninsula.

6 The River Tyne is in northern England and is 118 kilometres long. It is formed by the confluence of two rivers, the South Tyne and the North Tyne. The latter rises in the Scottish borders, and the former in Cumbria. The river flows from west to east into the North Sea.

7 The Romans called them "The Tattooed Ones" and considered them to be barbarians. The term is Greek and the word "barbarian" is derived from the Greek word "barbaros – βάρβάρος" found inscribed on clay tablets in Pylos in the region of Messenia circa 1200 BC. The word unambiguously denotes people who come from outside the city, who are strangers and alien, and C.P. Cavafy, in his poem "Waiting for the Barbarians", gives the word more ironic, contemporary connotations. Kostas Vlassopoulos, professor of history and archeology at the University of Crete, in his book *Greeks and*

Barbarians wrote "The barbarians are those who do not speak Greek" (Cambridge University Press 2013). Herodotus in *The Histories* describes the Persians, enemies of the Greeks, as "barbarians" on the grounds that they were a nation that spoke another (incomprehensible) language, but also because they were the enemy. But the term remained misleading.

We do not know precisely when the dramatic shift occurred, giving it its more explicitly negative connotations, as the Greek word was neutral, although perhaps it allowed for interpretation. The Romans, for their part, inherited the term from the Greeks and the meaning only changed for them when they became involved in violent wars against those who spoke a different language. The meaning came to include all foreigners who violated their borders and, since these barbarians were not remotely united, there were some who plundered the possessions of the Roman Empire and others who were allied with the Romans.

Then there were groups who shifted frequently between positions of hostility and friendship towards the Romans. Consequently, the term barbarian began to fluctuate to cover all the meanings, including people who were considered enemies of civilization from a civic perspective by the Greeks, and from an imperial perspective by the Romans. We will see below a compelling example in the character of Boudicca, who belonged to a Celtic tribe and was the wife of a king allied to the Romans, then became their arch enemy and fought them ferociously and ultimately became a legend in her own land of Britannia. See Walter Goffart,

Barbarian Tides. The Migration Age and the Later Roman Empire (Pennsylvania University Press, 2006).

8 Warriors of the tribes who fought the Romans and repeatedly targeted the garrisons of the Wall. These warrior tribes, originally composed of shepherds, hunters and peasants, were known for painting their faces and bodies, and tattooing them with colours in a semi-religious ritual, whose symbolism was related to the spirits of the ancestors.

9 A reference to a love relationship between the Emperor Hadrian and a young man from Thrace called Antinous, who was his favourite lover and accompanied him on his travels throughout the empire. The young man died during a voyage down the Nile in October, 130 CE. Historian Royston Lambert thinks it likely that the young man drowned, accidentally or otherwise. After his death Hadrian deified him, built temples for him, and founded a cult for his worship that spread throughout the empire. He established a city on the Nile called Antinoöpolis and sculptors filled the empire's cities with statues of him in response to his worshippers' demands. Archaeologists have found around two thousand statues of him, and he continued to be worshipped until the fourth century CE, when the emperor Theodosius put an end to the practice as he worked to eradicate pagan cults. In the eighteenth century Antinous re-emerged as a symbol of homosexuality in Europe. The appearance of a figurine in the possession of a young man became a secret sign of his sexual orientation, an invitation to another person of

the same orientation, according to Sarah Ann Waters, a Welsh novelist known for her Victorian themes and gay protagonists.

10 The eagle: emblem of the armies of the Roman Empire associated with victories, defeats and bloody events. The Romans were inspired by the ancient Syrians, who considered it as one of their symbols.

11 The Romans brought timber from the mountains of Numidia, an independent kingdom that was for a period a Roman province. It was built on parts of present-day Morocco, Algeria, Tunisia and Libya and its capital was Cirta (Constantine today). Cedar forests are widespread in the Atlas Mountains.

12 Baal: a Syrian deity first worshipped in the third mil-lennium BC in the Levant (Shām) and then around the ancient world in parts of present-day Asia, Europe and North Africa. In Aramaic and other Semitic languages it is a title or indefinite noun meaning master, lord or king, but Ugaritic texts show that Baal is a god with specific characteristics. Various records, including the Ugaritic texts, identify him as the god of weather, whose powers are associated with lightning, wind, rain, and fertility. The dry summer months in the region were interpreted as being caused by Baal's sojourn in the underworld, while his return in autumn accounted for the storms that renewed the land. Both Baal and El are associated with the bull in Ugaritic texts, as this animal symbolizes strength and fertility. The virgin goddess Anat is his older

sister and his wife. Baal was particularly hostile to snakes and serpents, whether they appeared as themselves or in the form of Yam, god of the sea and river. One of his most important functions in Ugaritic texts is the defence of humans and gods, as he is the hero of the gods and the slayer of the dragon Yam, the provider, the giver of rain whose voice, the thunder, is the promise of fertility, and the saviour who rules from Mount Saphon (Jabal Al-Aqra') in Syria.

His name is give in several different forms: *Alyan Baal*, the almighty, *Zebel Baal Ard*, the prince of the earth, *Baal Anat Muharth*, Baal of the ploughed land, and Hadad the god, or Young Hadad, or Baal the young prince. Baal is described as Son of Dagan, Baal of Tyre, later known as Melqart or king of the city, and is considered god of Damascus and Baalbek (Hadad is the Jupiter of Heliopolis – present-day Baalbek). He is also called Baal Shamim or Shamin, lord of heaven, and Baal Hadad, the Aramaic name which translates into the Greek Zeus.

He was seen by Canaanites and Phoenicians as the patron of sailors and seafaring merchants, a warrior god, god of the sun, and was also worshipped in Carthage in North Africa where he was called Baal Hammon. The name of the Carthaginian general Hannibal (Hana Baal) refers to his name, and the city of Baalbek in Syria (present-day Lebanon) also bears his name.

13 Asherah: a major goddess who occupies a prominent position among Syrian goddesses and in the myths of the ancient East. One of her functions is goddess of the sea, and she is the wife of El, the god of time. She gave birth

to seventy gods, among them Ishtar and Baal. From her name, we may infer that her worship is related to clan, and to social and conjugal relationships. Statues of her indicate clearly her female organs.

14 El: Canaanite deity, god of mankind and all creatures, god of gods. He fathered many gods, most importantly Hadad, Yam and Mot, each of whom shares attributes with the Greco-Roman deities Zeus, Poseidon and Hades. El is the counterpart of Zeus who is similarly considered the god of gods and mankind among the Greeks. According to the Ugaritic tablets, El is the husband of the goddess Asherah.

15 Archaeological studies indicate that in the second and third centuries AD, the Romans used skilled mariners from Mesopotamia, and perhaps specifically from Nineveh, who had exceptional experience of sailing small boats. They lived in the area of the Tyne by Hadrian's Wall, and their well-established presence there is confirmed by the fact that the fort where they were garrisoned was called at that time, and still is today, Arbeia.

16 The island of Delos (Greek: Δήλος), located near Mykonos in the centre of the Cyclades archipelago, is one of the most important cultural, mythological, historical and archaeological sites in Greece. It was a sacred site for the Greeks, as the birthplace of Apollo and Artemis, and Mount Cynthus on the island was believed to be the home of Zeus. In Roman times, the Greek islands, like

other parts of the Mediterranean, were a source of slaves as well as recruits for the Roman army.

17 The diverse ethnic and cultural affiliations that prevailed in the Roman army in the first, second, and third centuries AD meant that soldiers and junior officers were sometimes allowed to keep their national dress while on duty, as an acknowledgment of their cultural diversity. These forms of expression were most prominent at the time of Septimius Severus and the Syrian emperors who suceeded him.

18 Yabroud: Syrian city of major archaeological importance. Skulls dating back to the Stone Age have been found in its caves. It is located 77 km north of the Syrian capital, Damascus. In ancient times, it was a cultural centre mentioned on clay tablets from the era of Ashurbanipal, and in the writings of the Greek geographer Claudius Ptolemy. Its men were known to be hardy and resilient in war.

19 Reference to Jugurtha, the Numidian king who led some of the most famous wars against the Roman Empire. He was captured and taken to Rome, where he died in prison.

20 The capital of Numidia. The city of Constantine in the far east of Algeria stands on the same site today.

21 The god Baal Shamin, the great god of Tadmur or Palmyra.

22 The hymn here is inspired by the hymns offered to Baal in Syrian mythology: see the songs of Baal in other references to Syrian legends.

23 The city of Tadmur, in Latin 'Palmyra', and in Aramaic 'Tadmurta', meaning 'miracle'.

24 Tyre was a great city state and regional port next to the port of Sidon.

25 A reference to the Syrian poet Meliagros (Meleager) of Gadara, who lived in the first century BC and was a pioneer of the Syrian school of Greek poetry. He was a writer and collector of epigrams and himself wrote many satirical epigrams, now lost, as well as erotic sensual poetry, of which 134 epigrams have survived. He collected the poetry of his contemporaries and predecessors in an anthology entitled 'The Garland', which served as the basis for the *Greek Anthology*.

26 The Arab poet Imru' al-Qays was known as 'The Wanderer' because he spent his life seeking to revenge his father's death and to re-establish his father's lost kingdom.

27 Suha: a pale star in the 'Daughters of Na'sh' group of stars in the Ursa Major constellation, used by the ancient Arabs to test their eyesight. An Arab proverb says: 'I show her Suha and she shows me the moon', meaning 'I ask her something and she gives me an answer that has

nothing to do with my question'.

28 Suhail: a very bright star, associated with love by the ancient Arabs. The poet Abū al-ʿAlāʾ al-Maʿarrī said: Suhail is like the colour of love's cheek and the throbbing of the lover's heart.

29 Gaius Suetonius Paulinus (in Italian Gaio Svetonio Paolino), a Roman general best known for being the commander who defeated the Boudicca Rebellion (in around AD 60), was a consul and governor of Britannia.

30 Boudicca: queen of the Iceni tribe in Britannia (in Nero's time). She led one of the biggest rebellions against the Romans after she was deprived of the right to inherit the throne of her husband Prasutagus, the Iceni king. She was publicly flogged and her two daughters were raped in front of her. Although she and her forces killed thousands of Romans, she was eventually defeated in the famous battle of Watling Street. This took place in a valley with a forest behind it, a battle site more suitable for the Roman army, which was much smaller in number than her disorganized army. It is believed that after the battle she committed suicide, died of her wounds, or went into hiding.

31 The Aramaeans considered the rainbow to be a god.

32 One of the functions of the snake in the myths of the ancient East is as guardian of the waters, water being one of the basic substances of life. Consequently, snakes

and dragons have many functions in mythology, both good and evil.

33 A reference to the beetles that attacked Roman grain, caused great damage, and threatened a serious shortage of wheat supplies. The problem was sometimes dealt with by junior officers setting fire to the army's grain silos but more often Caledonian tribes were falsely accused of launching attacks from behind the Wall and sneaking in to light these fires just to cover their tracks.

34 The Celtic god of sacrifice who appears in the form of a woodcutter. It would be unworthy of a brave warrior with a god such as this to make a vile accusation.

35 There is an implication here that the consul's aide, the Calabrian youth, whose arrival from Rome may have been connected to the wheat supplies, was for some reason involved in the investigation into the fires lit to conceal the causes of the infestation of beetles.

36 The Itureans were known to be highly skilful archers and some of the fiercest fighters in the Roman batallions in eastern, central and western Europe. They formed a kind of mutually supportive sect and would not accept in their batallions – drawn from Damascus and the surrounding area as far as the city of Yabroud – anyone who was not an Iturean.

37 Woden / Odin in English, and in Norwegian Óðinn, a deity, or sacred ancestor, of the Caledonians, whom

they inherited from their distant Saxon roots.

He is mentioned in ancient manuscripts, including the rune poem dating back to the eighth or ninth century, and is associated with the magic of the nine herbs, and as a slayer of dragons and snakes. He has other functions and is considered the chief deity in Norse mythology. He is called the father of the gods, has many names, and is considered a god of wisdom, war and death, and also of magic, the unseen, poetry, victory and hunting. He can cause the dead to speak, in order to gain wisdom from the wisest of them. Two ravens, Huginn and Muninn (the old Norse words for thought and memory) fly around the world and bring him the latest news. He is one of the immortal gods and will eventually be killed by the wolf Fenrir, son of the god Loki, in the battle of the end of the world.

38 Julia Domna had a profound influence on Septimius Severus, the Libyan commander who headed the Roman armies in the east from his position in the north of Syria. She was the daughter of the High Priest of the Temple of Baal in Emesa (Homs in present-day Syria), born in 170 AD, well-educated and described as being very beautiful.

According to one of the many stories surrounding her, she was predicted by a fortune teller to bring success and happiness to the man who married her. Septimius lost no time in asking for Julia's hand from her father in 187 AD. He was 24 years older than her, born in Leptis Magna, the port city founded by Phoenicians in the 7th century BC (in present-day Libya), and was himself highly cultured. He studied literature and philosophy in Athens and worked as a lawyer in Rome. Historian Will Durant writes that despite his Semitic or Phoenician accent when he spoke Latin, he was one of the best-educated and most learned Romans of his time, and was eager to gather poets and philosophers around him. But he did not let philosophy deter him from fighting wars, nor allow poetry to soften his nature. Septimius Severus later became commander-in-chief of the Roman forces in Pannonia (present-day Hungary). Julia Domna bore him two sons, Caracalla (Qurrat Allah) and Geta, who were supposed to succeed their father as joint emperors. Shortly after their father's death, Geta was assassinated on Caracalla's orders.

39 The body of the emperor Severus was not cremated, but transported to Rome and buried there. In this poem he is cremated in accordance with an ancient Roman custom.

40 In the battles fought by Septimius Severus and his son Caracalla against the rebellious tribes of the Caledonians and others, the Romans provided about fifty thousand fighters, the vast majority of whom were non-Italians.

41 Or 'rider of the clouds': an epithet of Baal that recurs in songs and stories about him.

42 Epithets of two handmaids of the gods in Syrian mythology.

43 The reference here is derived from one of the chants of Baal and symbolizes the Tigris and Euphrates, reflected in the Tyne and the Thames.

44 A reference to the bearers of the emblem of the Roman eagle in their battle to regain this emblem after a failed encounter with the Caledonians, who believed that there were snakes in wells and canals where water flows, an ancient belief shared by many peoples.

45 According to Palmyrene beliefs there are seven jinn gods whose function is to act as mediators between the major gods and human beings, as well as being protectors of the city. A sculpture of them all together, dating back to the year 181 AD, was found in the remains of a temple in Jabal Sha'ir near Palmyra. They are: Salman, Abjal, Ma'n, Sa'd, al-Raji', Asher, Mun'im, with their sister Salma. These names are present in the Arabic lexicon and some of them are still in circulation today, such as Salman, Saad, Mun'im, Ma'n and Salma.

46 Lenus: a Celtic god of healing.

47 Maponus: a god of music and poetry in Celtic Britain, equivalent to Apollo, Greek god of the arts.

48 Allat: literally "the goddess". A pre-Islamic Arabian goddess, one of the three chief goddesses of Mecca, and the major goddess of Tadmur [Palmyra], considered by pre-Islamic Arabs as one of Allah's three daughters.

49 Saitada: Celtic goddess from the Tyne Valley, known as the goddess of grief.

50 Baniyas: an ancient port in Syria.

51 Morrigan: a goddess of war who appears in the form of a crow.

52 Odin: a god of northern European origin. See note 37 above.

53 Iceni: a powerful British Celtic tribe, led by Boudicca after the death of her husband, the king of the Iceni.

54 Agricola: eminent Roman general responsible for much of the Roman conquest of Britain. His son-in-law, the famous historian Tacitus, wrote Agricola's life story and it is thanks to his account that we have information about Boudicca.

55 Many threads connect Alexander to Antinous. Both men are associated with the River Nile. Antinous drowned in the Nile and Alexander conquered Egypt. Alexander ordered the minting of coins depicting himself standing by the Nile with his foot on the crocodile that was a symbol of the Nile in Egypt. The precise whereabouts of Alexander's tomb is not known and the drowned body of Antinous was never found. Finally, in the eyes of Hadrian and a number of Roman emperors, Alexander was a hero for both his military prowess and intellectual and emotional qualities, and possibly also as a

homosexual icon.

56 These youths may be assistants to priests whose work includes embalming and writing, and the pots are for mixing henna and inks and dyes and other materials used for embalming the dead and writing on the wood of coffins and on papyrus tablets.

57 The king's entertainment here refers to the rituals associated with recreational excursions into the countryside, visits to architectural monuments, military parades and "processions of the sun", festivals held in boats on the Nile. These are pharaonic rituals and customs, many of which were inherited by the Ptolemies. The pharaoh or king was usually accompanied by the queen, princesses, courtiers, writers, athletes, musicians, engineers, priests and others whose presence he desired.

58 *The Ruin*: the title given to a poetic elegy believed to have been written in England between the eighth and tenth centuries. This is a rare poetic relic in Old English by an anonymous poet lamenting the destroyed buildings of a beautiful Roman city, thought to be Bath, which was built by the Romans. The edge of the parchment on which the poem was written was burnt, and so part of the text was lost.

59 Julia Domna lost a number of her fingers when her younger son, Geta, ran to her for protection from the soldiers sent by his brother Caracalla to assassinate him.

60 The agora was the square where peasants and philosophers used to meet in Athens from the 5th century BC. It was the gathering place for those wanting to hear statements, declarations and edicts issued by kings and councils of elders, and the public space where fundamental resolutions were adopted in ancient Greek society, as well as in the eastern metropolises of the Hellenistic period, like Palmyra, Damascus, Alexandria, Rome and other major cities. The agora was also the place where people went to enlist in the army. Slaves and maids were not allowed to frequent the agora. In later times it became the biggest commercial centre and the heart of the city and eventually formed an administrative, religious and commercial centre for the entire state. The idea of the agora evolved later on when it attracted craftsmen and their workshops and small traders' kiosks and became like the 'downtown' of today.

61 The reference is to Queen Zenobia of Palmyra, who lost her war with the Roman empire, and her kingdom, and according to some sources spent her last days under house arrest in Hadrian's villa in Rome.

RELATED REFERENCES

Links to archaeological and historical sources about Regina's funerary tablet, discovered in 1878 near the Roman fort of Arbeia, in present-day South Shields. These writings study the monument from many linguistic and historical angles, investigate the different possibilities regarding the identities of Regina and Barates, and also bring to light more about the nature of its connection to the geographical space of both the Roman fort and Hadrian's Wall:

The Aleppo Project, 'A Celtic Queen and Her Syrian Husband'. Accessed 18th December 2021.
https://www.thealeppoproject.com/a-celtic-queen-and-her-syrian-husband/

Beth, C. 'Weekend Reading: Visiting Regina'
https://classicalstudies.support/2018/09/07/weekend-reading-visiting-regina/

Burke, E. 'Barates and Regina: An ancient love story'. Accessed 18th December 2021:
https://slideplayer.com/slide/8034675/

Cecil, C. O. 'Hadrian's Syrians'. Accessed 18th December 2021. https://www.aramcoworld.com/Articles/July-2017/Hadrian-s-Syrians-1

Jones, P. 'Regina, a Syrian in South Shields', *The Spectator*, 16 December 2017.

Panofsky, E. 'Barates at the End of The World'. Accessed 18th December 2021.
https://havechanged.blogspot.com/2018/02/barates-at-end-of-world.html

Stuchbery, M. 'As Epic as Jon Snow and Daenerys – a Glimpse of Roman Britain's Multicultural Love', *Byline Times*, 9 May 2019.
https://bylinetimes.com/2019/05/09/as-epic-as-jon-snow-and-daenerys-a-glimpse-of-roman-britains-multi cultural-love/

Warwick Classics Network, 'Regina of Arbeia'. Accessed 18th December 2021.
https://warwick.ac.uk/fac/arts/classics/warwickclassicsnet work/romancoventry/resources/diversity/women/regina/

Weingarten, J. 'The Little Queen at Hadrian's Wall', 14 August 2011.
http://judithweingarten.blogspot.com/2011/08/little-queen-at-hadrians-wall.html

ACKNOWLEDGEMENTS

This translation would not have been possible without the support and encouragement that Margaret Obank and Samuel Shimon gave to every line when they took it on at Banipal. I am profoundly grateful that they chose a first-rate translator, Catherine Cobham, to render this work into English, a matter of enduring pride for me.

For the key poem of this book I am indebted to Khaldoun al-Shamaa, Abd al-Rahman Bisisu, and Mufid Nejm, respected critics who read the text and gave me their impressions. Their passion for epic poetry strengthened my certainty of the need for the work to come out as soon as possible. For inspiring me with confidence in my poetry when I was lacking it, they deserve the highest appreciation.

NOURI AL-JARRAH

Nouri al-Jarrah was born in Damascus in 1956. He attracted attention with his debut collection of poems, *The Boy*, published in Beirut in 1982 and has become an influential poetic voice on the Arab literary scene. Since 1986 he has lived in London, publishing 16 further collections, and founding and editing a number of Arabic literary magazines. Very much a performance poet, he travels widely around the world to festivals and book fairs, reading his latest works and supporting their translations into other languages.

His poetry draws on diverse cultural sources, and is marked by a special focus on mythology, folk tales and legends. Selected poems have been translated into a number of Asian and European languages, and some collections have been published in French, Spanish and Farsi.

A Boat to Lesbos and other Poems (Banipal Books, 2018) was his first collection in English translation, joining the original Arabic book's translations into French, Spanish, Turkish, Italian, Greek and Farsi.

CATHERINE COBHAM

Catherine Cobham taught Arabic language and literature at the University of St Andrews, Scotland, for many years, and has translated works of a number of Arab writers, including poetry by Adonis, Mahmoud Darwish, Ghayath Almadhoun and Tammam Hunaidy, and novels and short stories by Naguib Mahfouz, Yusuf Idris, Hanan al-Shaykh and Fuad al-Takarli.

TITLES FROM
BANIPAL BOOKS

The Stone Serpent, Barates of Palmyra's Elegy for Regina his Beloved – An Eastern Serenade by Nouri Al-Jarrah. Translated from the Arabic by Catherine Cobham. ISBN: 978-1-913043-29-2 • 2022 • 112pp • Pbk & Ebook. Syrian poet Al-Jarrah restores to life an ancient story of migrant Syrian life, love and freedom, the story of Barates of Palmyra and Regina the Celt, after a single line in Aramaic on a tombstone at Arabeia Roman Fort, Hadrian's Wall, fired his imagination.

Things I Left Behind by Shada Mustafa. Translated from the Arabic by Nancy Roberts. ISBN: 978-1-913043-26-1 • 2022 • 128pp • Pbk & Ebook. This debut novel by a young Palestinian woman interrogates the memories of growing up in order to find liberation from the continual pain and tragic anguish of the "things" she left behind in her childhood in an occupied and divided land and family.

The Tent Generations, Palestinian Poems. Selected, introduced, and translated by Mohammed Sawaie. ISBN: 978-1-913043-18-6 • 2022 • 160pp • Pbk & Ebook. These Palestinian poets, most in English for the first time, bear witness, through their experiences of displacement, disapora and occupation, to the *Nakba* of 1948, 1967, 1973 and beyond.

Sarajevo Firewood by Saïd Khatibi. Translated from the Arabic by Paul Starkey. ISBN 978-1-913043-23-0 • 2021 • 320pp • Pbk & Ebook. This unusual novel explores the legacy of recent histories, connections and civil wars of Algeria and Bosnia-Herzegovina with the traumatic experience of exile for so many. A fictional memorial to the thousands of dead and disappeared, as well as survivors.

Shortlisted for the 2020 International Prize for Arabic Fiction.

Fadhil Al-Azzawi's Beautiful Creatures by Iraqi author Fadhil al-Azzawi. ISBN 978-1-913043-10-0 • 2021 • 152pp • Hbk, Pbk, Ebook. Translated from the Arabic by the author, and edited by Hannah Somerville. This poetic open work was written in defiance of the "sanctity of genre" and to raise the question of freedom of expression in writing. First published in Arabic in 1969 to great acclaim, it has been variously called a novel or a prose poem, while the author calls it an epic in prose, divided as it is into cantos.

The Madness of Despair by Ghalya F T Al Said. Translated from the Arabic by Raphael Cohen. ISBN: 978-1-913043-12-4 • 2021 • 256pp • Hbk, Pbk, Ebook. The first of the author's six novels to be published in English is a powerful saga of just how much psychological suffering and cultural displacement can upset the most ordinary of aspirations for life and love.

Poems of Alexandria and New York by Ahmed Morsi. Translated from the Arabic by Raphael Cohen. ISBN 978-1-913043-16-2 • 2021 • 126pp • Pbk & Ebook. The poet's first volume in English translation, it captures the modernity that is at the heart of all his works, his surrealistic humour, and his visions of the dramas of ordinary life. It comprises two of his many collections, Pictures from the New York Album and Elegies to the Mediterranean, both written when he resumed writing poetry following a break of nearly 30 years.

Mansi: A Rare Man in His Own Way by Tayeb Salih. Translated and introduced by Adil Babikir. ISBN 978-0-9956369-8-9 • Pbk & Ebook • 184pp • 2020. This affectionate memoir of Salih's irrepressible friend Mansi shows a new side to the author, known worldwide for his classic novel *Season of Migration to the North*.

Goat Mountain by Habib Selmi.Translated from the Arabic by Charis Olszok. ISBN: 978-1-913043-04-9 • 2020 • Pbk

& Ebook • 92pp. The well-known Tunisian author's debut novel, from 1988, now in English translation. "*I enjoyed this book. I liked its gloomy atmosphere, its strangeness . . . Eerie, funereal, and outstanding!*" – Jabra Ibrahim Jabra

The Mariner by Taleb Alrefai. Translated from the Arabic by Russell Harris. ISBN: 978-1-913043-08-7 • Pbk & Ebook • 160pp • 2020. A fictional re-telling of the final treacherous journey at sea of famous Kuwaiti dhow shipmaster Captain Al-Najdi, with flashbacks to the awesome pull of the sea on Al-Najdi since childhood, his voyages around the Arabian Peninsula with Australian sailor Alan Villiers, and the demise of pearl-fishing.

A Boat to Lesbos, and other poems by Nouri Al-Jarrah. Translated from the Arabic by Camilo Gómez-Rivas and Allison Blecker and illustrated with paintings by Reem Yassouf. ISBN: 978-0-9956369-4-1 • 2018 • Pbk • 120pp. The first book in English translation for this major Syrian poet, bearing passionate witness – through the eye of history, of Sappho and the travels of Odysseus – to Syrian families fleeing to Lesbos.

An Iraqi In Paris by Samuel Shimon. ISBN: 978-0-9574424-8-1 • Pbk • 282pp • 2016. Translated from the Arabic by Christina Philips and Piers Amodia with the author. Called by critics: "a gem of autobiographical writing", "a manifesto of tolerance", "a cinematographic odyssey".

Heavenly Life: Selected Poems by Ramsey Nasr. ISBN: 978-0-9549666-9-0 • 2010 • Pbk • 180pp. First English-language collection for Ramsey Nasr, Poet Laureate of the Netherlands 2009 & 2010. Translated from the Dutch by David Colmer. Introduced by Victor Schiferli with Foreword by Ruth Padel.

Knife Sharpener: Selected Poems by Sargon Boulus. The first English-language collection for the influential and innovative late Iraqi poet. ISBN: 978-0-9549666-7-6 • 2009 • Pbk • 154pp. Foreword by Adonis. Poems translated from the Arabic by the author. Plus tributes by fellow authors and publisher's Afterword.

Shepherd of Solitude: Selected Poems by Amjad Nasser. Translated from the Arabic and introduced by Khaled Mattawa. ISBN: 978-0-9549666-8-3 • 2009 • Pbk • 186pp. First English-language collection for the late major Jordanian poet, poems selected from the years 1979 to 2004.

Mordechai's Moustache and his Wife's Cats, and other stories by short story maestro Mahmoud Shukair. ISBN: 978-0-9549666-3-8 • 2007 • Pbk • 124pp. Translated from the Arabic by Issa J Boullata, Elizabeth Whitehouse, Elizabeth Winslow and Christina Phillips. First major publication in English of Palestine's most original of storytellers.

A Retired Gentleman, & other stories by Issa J Boullata. ISBN: 978-0-9549666-6-9 • 2007 • Pbk • 120pp. The Jerusalem-born author, scholar, and translator presents a rich medley of emigrant tales.

The Myrtle Tree by Lebanese Jad El Hage. ISBN: 978-0-9549666-4-5 • 2007 • Pbk • 288pp. "This remarkable novel, set in a Lebanese mountain village, conveys with razor-sharp accuracy the sights, sounds, tastes and tragic dilemmas of Lebanon's fratricidal civil war. A must read" – Patrick Seale.

Sardines and Oranges: Short Stories from North Africa. Introduced by Peter Clark. ISBN: 978-0-9549666-1-4 • 2005 • Pbk • 222pp. The 26 stories from Algeria, Egypt, Morocco, Sudan and Tunisia are by 21 authors, all translated from the Arabic, bar one, Mohammed Dib's from French.